I0797587

ANIMALS WITH SUPERPOWERS!

DEFEND AND ATTACK!

WRITTEN BY
EMILIE DUFRESNE
DESIGNED BY AMY LI

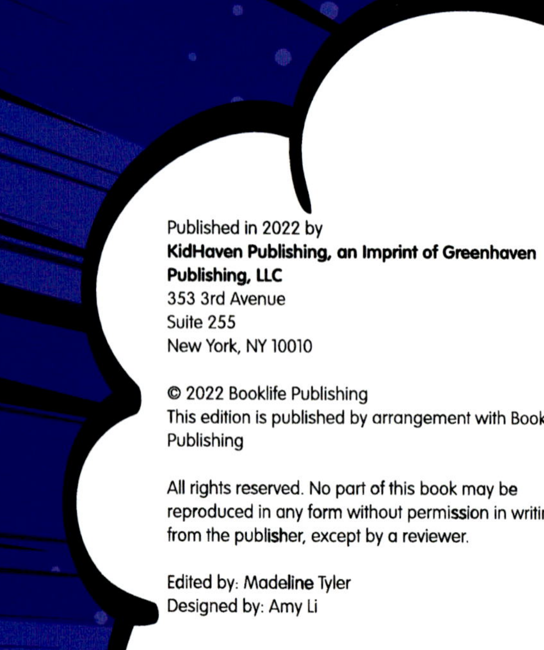

Published in 2022 by
KidHaven Publishing, an Imprint of Greenhaven Publishing, LLC
353 3rd Avenue
Suite 255
New York, NY 10010

Edited by: Madeline Tyler
Designed by: Amy Li

Find us on

Cataloging-in-Publication Data

Names: Dufresne, Emilie.
Title: Defend and attack! / Emilie Dufresne.
Description: New York : KidHaven Publishing, 2022. | Series: Animals with superpowers! | Includes glossary and index.
Identifiers: ISBN 9781534535053 (pbk.) | ISBN 9781534535077 (library bound) | ISBN 9781534535060 (6 pack) | ISBN 9781534535084 (ebook)
Subjects: LCSH: Animal weapons--Juvenile literature. | Animal defenses--Juvenile literature.
Classification: LCC QL759.D847 2022 | DDC 591.47--dc23

Printed in the United States of America

CPSIA compliance information: Batch #CS22KH: For further information contact Greenhaven Publishing LLC, New York, New York at 1-844-317-7404.

Please visit our website, www.greenhavenpublishing.com. For a free color catalog of all our high-quality books, call toll free 1-844-317-7404 or fax 1-844-317-7405.

PHOTO CREDITS *All images courtesy of Shutterstock. With thanks to Getty Images, Thinkstock Photo, and iStockphoto.*
Cover – Azamatovic, Lazerko A, UltraViolet, Zorana Matijasevic, Tiny Doz. Vector Animals – natchapohn, Andrew Rybalko (Professor Ax), Guz Anna (Hedgehog), natchapohn (eel, scorpion), StockSmartStart (skunk, bull, narwhal, shrimp). Master images – TinyDoz (header font), Azamatovic, Natalisa (main and panel backgrounds), Zorana Matijasevic, UltraViolet (Comic bubbles, assets and annotations), Nata Alhontess (Speech bubbles and boxes), Lazerko A (page number cloud, stars). 1 – Lazerko A, 2-3 – Nata Alhontess, 4-5 – james weston, 6-7 – lukpedclub, teekayu, Mikhail Cheremkin, enjoy your life, A7880S, 8-9 – Lanaart, Alexandr III, Eric Isslee, 10-11 – Anna Violet, Eric Isslee, Guz Anna, Anna Frajtova, 12-13 – Baksiabat, StockSmartStart, By NPavelN, Catmando, Ralko, 14-15 – Yauhen Paleski, Panda Vector, Anna Frajtova, kstudija, Sanit_Fuangnakhon, d_odin, 16-17 – Guz Anna, wacpan, VitaliyVill, Jiw Ingka, 18-19 – Baksiabat, world of vector, Pikepicture, Nichole Casebolt, 20-21 – Baksiabat, StockSmartStart, Claudia Pylinskaya, Matthew R McClure, vasilchuk, jehomwang, the8monkey, Andrew Rybalko, 22-23– james weston, mhatzapa.

CONTENTS

PAGE 4 Superheroes of the Future
PAGE 6 Mega Weapons
PAGE 8 Hedgehogs
PAGE 10 Skunks
PAGE 12 Narwhals
PAGE 14 Bulls
PAGE 16 Scorpions
PAGE 18 Electric Eels
PAGE 20 Pistol Shrimps
PAGE 22 The Next Generation
PAGE 24 Glossary and Index

Words that look like **this** can be found in the glossary on page 24.

SUPERHEROES OF THE FUTURE

The world is constantly under threat. Whether it's from crime, alien invasions, or humans destroying the planet, one thing is known for certain. Something has got to change...

A new generation of superheroes is needed to protect the planet.
Join me, Professor Ax, as I search high and low for the superheroes of the future. There's no time to lose – let's get started!

MEGA WEAPONS

Attack Weapons

These animals all have amazing weapons that either help them defend and protect themselves, or attack other animals.

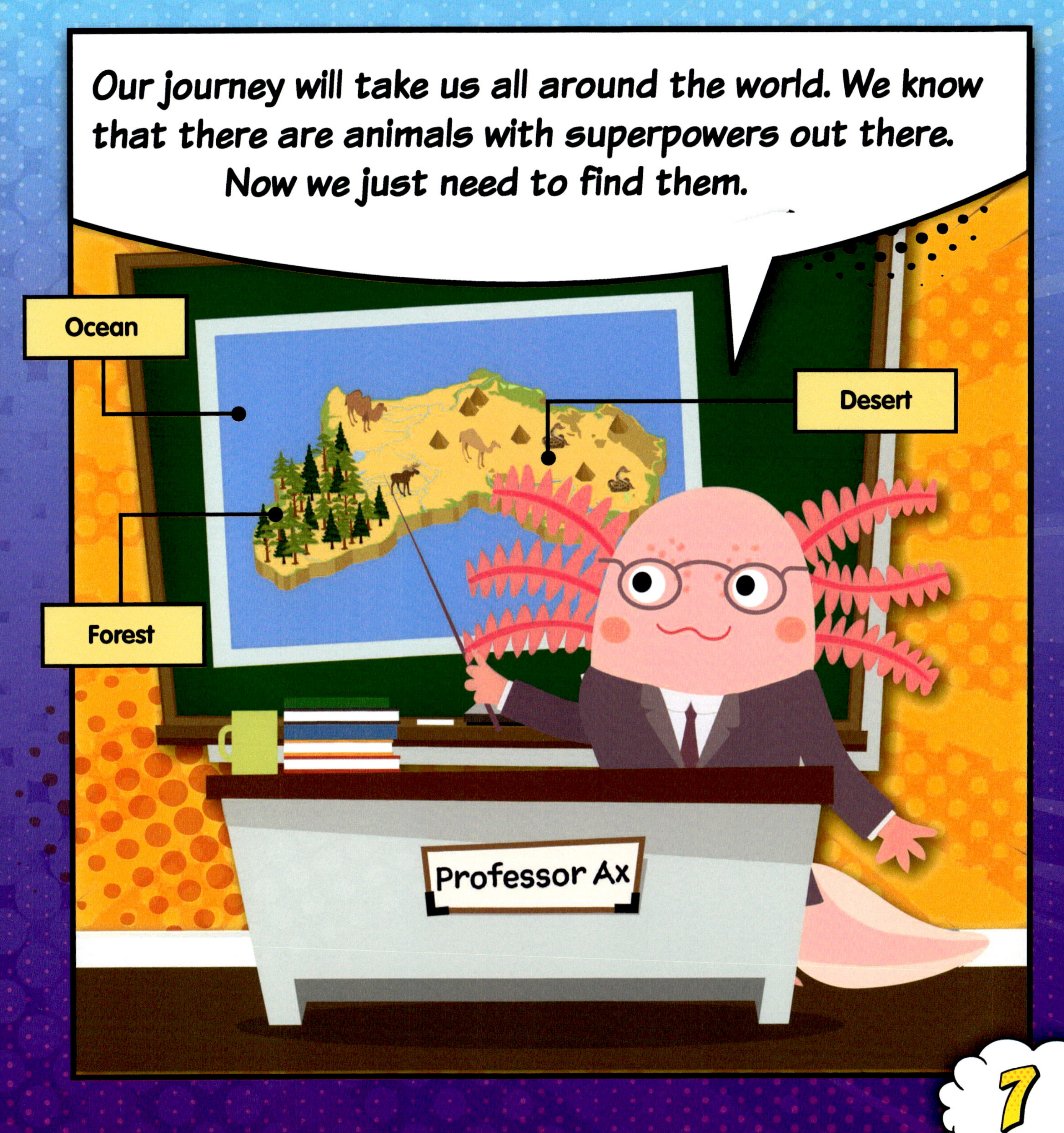
Our journey will take us all around the world. We know that there are animals with superpowers out there. Now we just need to find them.
Ocean
Desert
Forest
Professor Ax

HEDGEHOGS
Hedgehogs might look like cute animals, but they have devious defense weapons...
Uh-oh...
Whenever they feel threatened by a predator, all they have to do is roll into a ball and...

...up to **5,000** quills are raised and make the hedgehog a spiky, scary ball that predators find very difficult to attack.

ZOOM

The coast is clear. You can come out now.

No chance!

NAME:	Hedgehog
LIVES:	Europe, Asia, and Africa
SIZE:	Up to 11.8 inches (30 cm) long
SUPERPOWER:	Can turn into a ball of spikes whenever needed

SKUNKS
These nocturnal creatures hold a powerful defensive weapon in the most unlikely place...
Under their tails, they have special glands near their bum that can shoot out a stinky liquid to scare off any predators nearby.
SPLAT!
Does something smell, or is it just me?
10

Not only does this liquid stink, but it clings to the skin and fur of the predator and can travel over 9.8 feet (3 m) through the air.

I'm going to eat that tasty skunk!

WATCH OUT!

Wow, you stink!

NAME:	Skunk
LIVES:	Most common in North and South America
SIZE:	Around 27.6 inches (70 cm), including tail
SUPERPOWER:	Covering predators with stinky spray

NARWHALS
These mythical-looking creatures have an amazing weapon and tool. The horn coming out of their head is actually a very long tooth!
This tooth can be used as a weapon to hit and stun their prey, so that they are easier to eat.

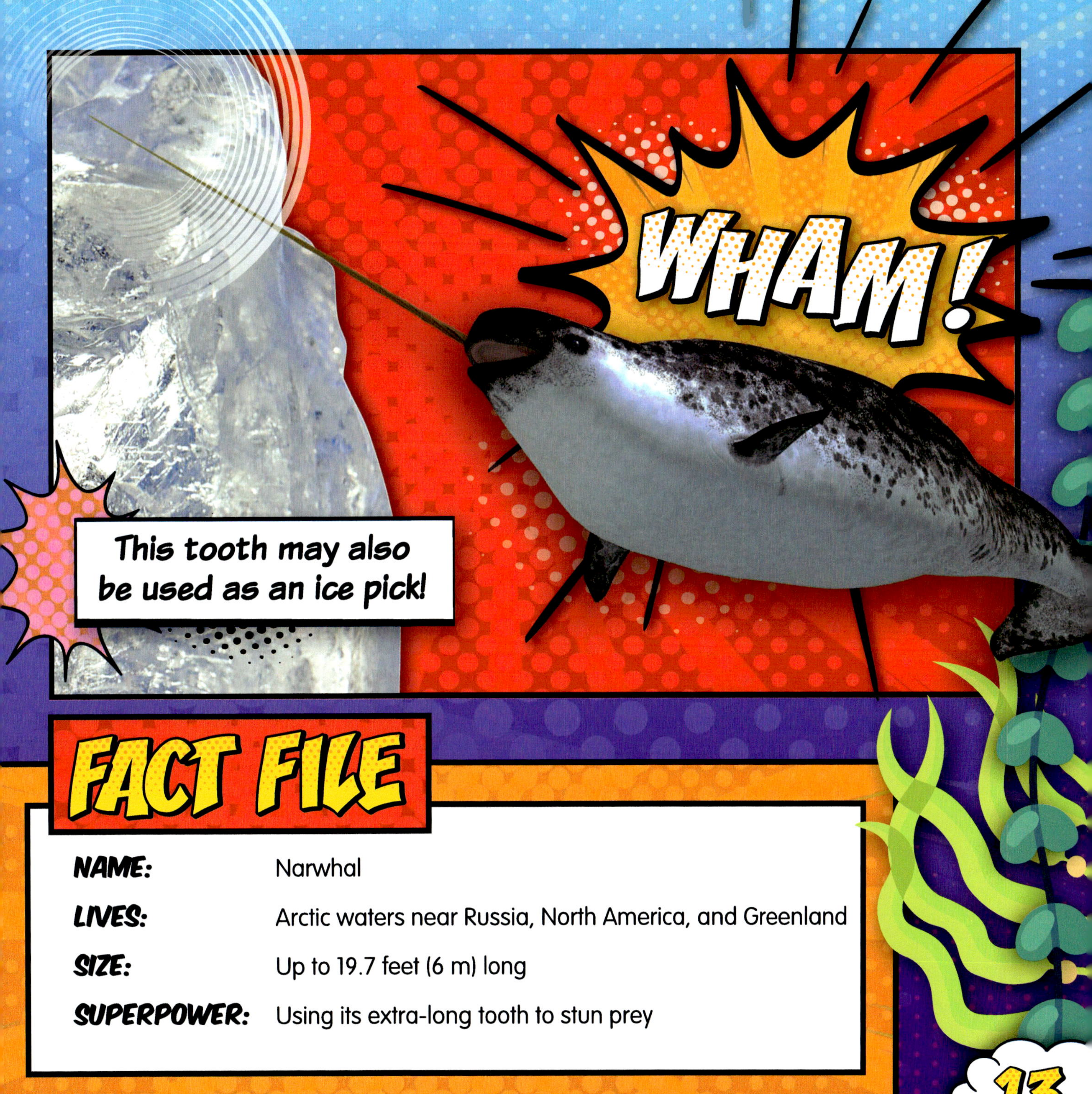

FACT FILE

NAME:	Narwhal
LIVES:	Arctic waters near Russia, North America, and Greenland
SIZE:	Up to 19.7 feet (6 m) long
SUPERPOWER:	Using its extra-long tooth to stun prey

Bulls have very large horns. They **charge** at other bulls with their horns to show their **dominance**. Bulls are usually very muscly and strong.

You won't like me when I'm angry!

The horns are attached to the bull's skull. They are very strong and are perfect for fighting.

Bulls' horns are made of the same thing as your fingernails!

Bull Horns

FACT FILE

NAME:	Bull
LIVES:	Worldwide
SIZE:	Up to 1,540 pounds (700 kg) in weight
SUPERPOWER:	Using its horns and strength to show its dominance

SCORPIONS
BUZZZzzz!
BUZZZzzz!
Scorpions are known for their deadly stingers. They hold their prey with their pincers so that they can't get away.
Stinger
They use their stingers to inject powerful venom into their prey to stop it from moving.
Pincers

Their stings are so deadly that some can even **kill** humans!

NAME:	Indian red scorpion
LIVES:	Common in India, Pakistan, and Nepal
SIZE:	Up to 4.7 inches (12 cm)
SUPERPOWER:	A stinger packed with powerful venom

ELECTRIC EELS

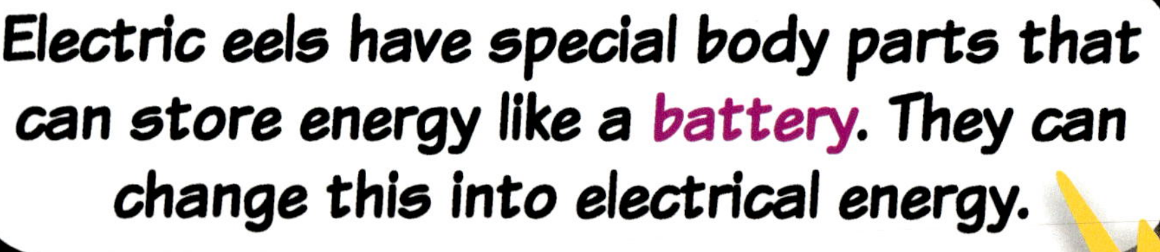

Electric eels have special body parts that can store energy like a **battery**. They can change this into electrical energy.

I have a shocking superpower!

They can shoot out electricity to stun any predators or prey nearby.

FACT FILE

NAME:	Electric eel	**SIZE:**	Up to 8.2 feet (2.5 m) long
LIVES:	Streams and ponds in South America	**SUPERPOWER:**	Killing prey using electricity

PISTOL SHRIMPS

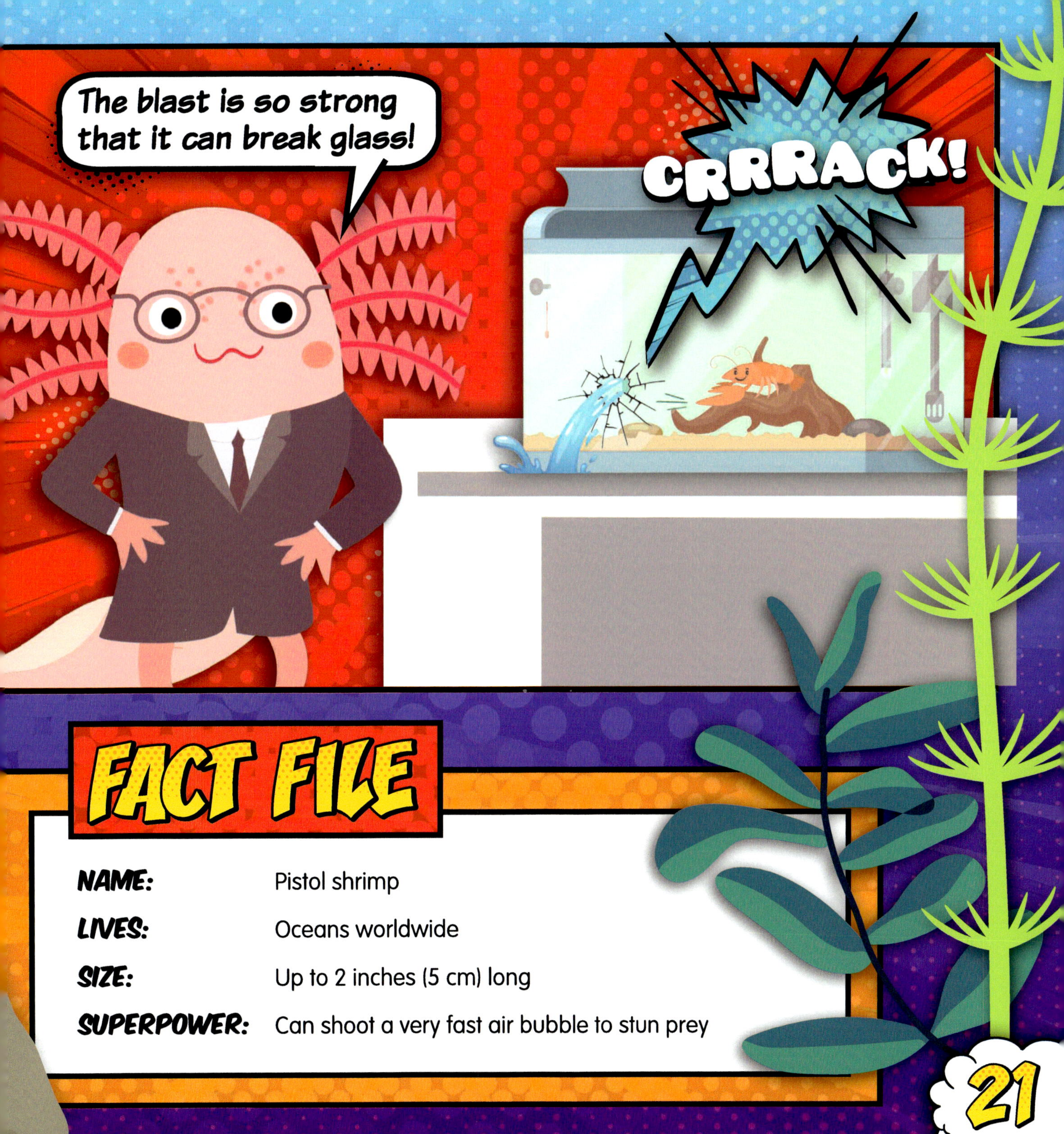

FACT FILE

NAME: Pistol shrimp

LIVES: Oceans worldwide

SIZE: Up to 2 inches (5 cm) long

SUPERPOWER: Can shoot a very fast air bubble to stun prey

THE NEXT
GENERATION
SHRIMP SHOT
STINK IN THE NIGHT
TOOTHPICK
All of these animals are now ready to join my team, but first they need their superhero identities! Remember these faces; they might save the world one day!
A
RED DEATH

ARE YOU A MEGA WEAPON SUPERHERO?
Humans have one of the best mega weapons around – their brains! Think about all the ways we use our brains to plan ahead, work as a team, and understand consequences.
TWO-PRONGED ATTACK
AQUATIC SHOCK
SPIKE

GLOSSARY

battery	a device that stores energy
charge	to run with full strength at something
dominance	to be the strongest or most important within a group
generation	a group of people that are of a similar age and involved in a particular activity
glands	organs in the body that produce chemical substances for the body to use
inject	to push a liquid into something using a needle-like object
mythical	relating to myths or legends
nocturnal	active at night instead of during the day
predator	an animal that hunts other animals for food
prey	animals that are hunted by other animals for food
quills	sharp hollow spikes on animals such as hedgehogs and porcupines
stun	to make unconscious by using a blow or shock
venom	a harmful substance that is injected through a bite or a sting

INDEX

America 11, 13, 19
Arctic 13
bums 10
claws 20
electricity 18–19
Europe 9
generation 5, 22
ice 13
liquid 10–11
nocturnal 10
oceans 7, 21
pincers 16
quills 9
stingers 16–17
teeth 12–13